AF094587

Celebrating The Marriage

&

_____

On: _____

At: _____

They Are No Longer Two, But One

Our Guests

Our Guests

Our Guests

Our Guests

Our Guests

Our Guests

Our Guests

Our Guests

Our Guests

Our Guests

Our Guests

Our Guests

Our Guests

Our Guests

Our Guests

Our Guests

Our Guests

Our Guests

Our Guests

Our Guests

Our Guests

Our Guests

Our Guests

Our Guests

Our Guests

Our Guests

Our Guests

Our Guests

Our Guests

Our Guests

Our Guests

Our Guests

Our Guests

Our Guests

Our Guests

Our Guests

Our Guests

Our Guests

Our Guests

Our Guests

Our Guests

Our Guests

Our Guests

Our Guests

Our Guests

Our Guests

Our Guests

Our Guests

Our Guests

Our Guests

Our Guests

Our Guests

Our Guests

Our Guests

Our Guests

Our Guests

Our Guests

Our Guests

Our Guests

Our Guests

Our Guests

Our Guests

Our Guests

Our Guests

Our Guests

Our Guests

Our Guests

Our Guests

Our Guests

Our Guests

Our Guests

Our Guests

Our Guests

Our Guests

Our Guests

Our Guests

Our Guests

Our Guests

Our Guests

Our Guests

Our Guests

Our Guests

Our Guests

Our Guests

Our Guests

Our Guests

Our Guests

Our Guests

Our Guests

Our Guests

Our Guests

Our Guests

Our Guests

Our Guests

Our Guests

Our Guests

Our Guests

Our Guests

Our Guests

www.ingramcontent.com/pod-product-compliance
Lightning Source LLC
LaVergne TN
LVHW060335080526
838202LV00053B/4478